100
things you should know about
PYRAMIDS

100
things you should know about
PYRAMIDS

John Malam
Consultant: Fiona Macdonald

MC
PUBLISHERS

This 2009 edition published and distributed by:
Mason Crest Publishers Inc.
370 Reed Road, Broomall, Pennsylvania 19008
(866) MCP-BOOK (toll free)
www.masoncrest.com

Library of Congress Cataloging-in-Publication data is available
100 Things You Should Know About Pyramids
ISBN 978-1-4222-1525-8

100 Things You Should Know About - 10 Title Series
ISBN 978-1-4222-1517-3

Printed in the United States of America
9 8 7 6 5 4 3 2

First published as hardback in 2008 by Miles Kelly Publishing Ltd
Bardfield Centre, Great Bardfield, Essex, CM7 4SL

ACKNOWLEDGEMENTS
The publishers would like to thank the following artists
who have contributed to this book:
Mike Foster, Adam Hook, Richard Hook, Colin Livingstone,
Patricia Ludlow, Carlo Molinari, Giuseppe Rava
All other artworks are from the Miles Kelly Artwork Bank

The publishers would like to thank the following sources
for the use of their photographs:
Page 6 M. Crame/Alamy; 10 JTB Photo/Photolibrary; 11 Walter Rawlings/Alamy;
15 Roger Ressmeyer/Corbis; 21 Werner Forman/TopFoto; 22 Richard T. Nowitz/Corbis;
31 Benjamin Lowy/Corbis; 36 Blaine Harrington III/Alamy; 37 (t) Jeremy Horner/Corbis, (b) World Pictures/Alamy;
40 Mike Nelson/epa/Corbis; 41 Kevin Schafer/Corbis; 42 2006 Alinari/TopFoto; 44 Stuart Clark/Rex Features;
45 (t) Elma Okic/Rex Features, (b) Homer Sykes/Corbis; 46 James Osmond/Alamy

All other photographs are from:
Corel, digitalSTOCK, digitalvision, iStockphoto.com, John Foxx, PhotoAlto,
PhotoDisc, PhotoEssentials, PhotoPro, Stockbyte

Contents

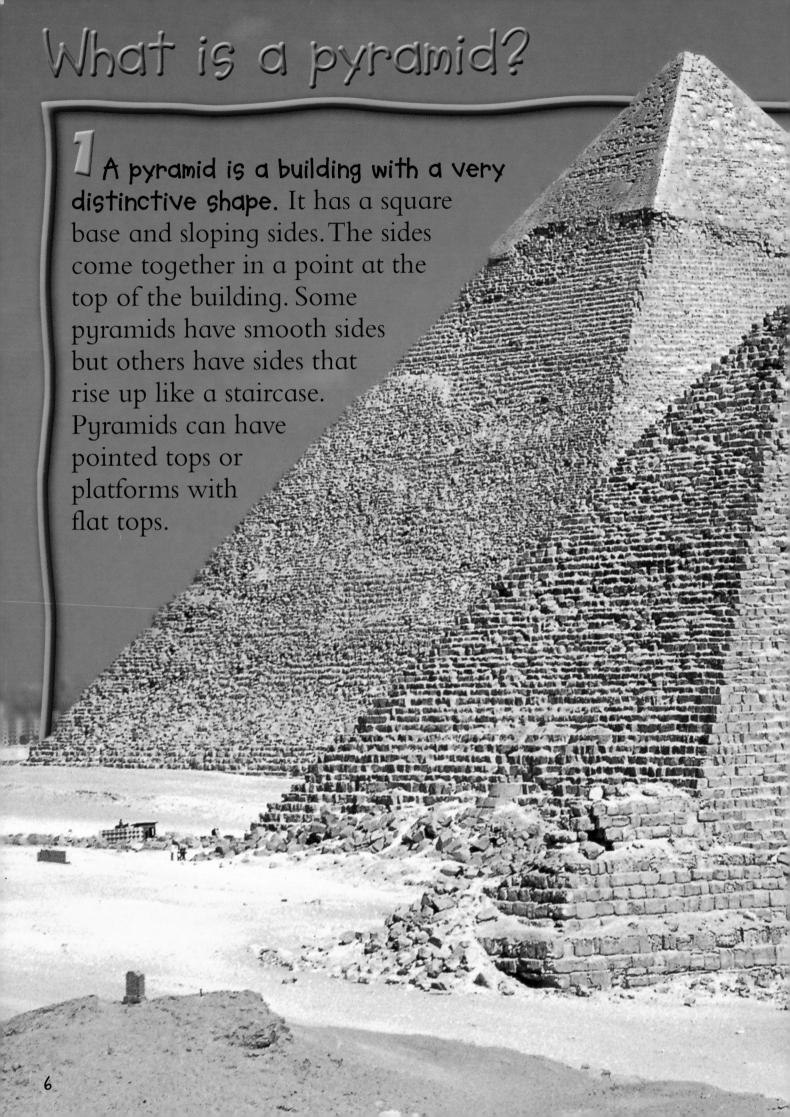

What is a pyramid?

1 **A pyramid is a building with a very distinctive shape.** It has a square base and sloping sides. The sides come together in a point at the top of the building. Some pyramids have smooth sides but others have sides that rise up like a staircase. Pyramids can have pointed tops or platforms with flat tops.

The pyramids of Giza in Egypt are the best-known pyramids in the world. They were built about 4500 years ago. The three biggest pyramids were tombs for ancient Egyptian kings. In front of them are three small pyramids, which were tombs for other members of the royal family.

The pyramid sites of ancient Egypt are all situated along the river Nile.

KEY
1. Giza
2. Saqqara
3. Dahshur
4. Meidum
5. Valley of the kings

SYRIA

Nile Delta

LIBYA

NUBIA

River Nile

Egypt – land of pyramids

① Pit burial

Mound of sand over pit

Dead person with grave goods

At first, bodies were buried in pits (1). Later on, the pits were covered with mud-brick platforms, or mastabas (2). Finally, several platforms were put on top of each other to make the first pyramid – the Step Pyramid (3).

3 **The ancient Egyptians didn't suddenly decide to start building pyramids.** Around 3100 BCE there was a change in the way important people were buried. Instead of burying them in holes in the desert, they were buried in underground tombs carved into the rock. A low platform of mud-brick was built over the tomb, called a mastaba.

Mud-brick platform

② Mastaba

Graves below ground surface

2 **The word 'pyramid' was introduced to the English language by the ancient Greeks.** They saw that Egyptian loaves were a similar shape to Egypt's huge buildings. The Greeks called Egyptian loaves 'pyramides', meaning 'wheat cakes'. In time, this word changed into the English word 'pyramid'.

③ Step Pyramid

Underground passages and chambers

4 **Pyramids developed from mastabas.**
The first pyramid was built for Djoser, one of the first Egyptian pharaohs (kings). It began as a mastaba, but was built from stone instead of mud-brick. A second platform was added on top of the mastaba, followed by a smaller one on top of that. The mound grew until it had six platforms. It looked like an enormous staircase, which is why it is known as the Step Pyramid.

QUIZ

1. How many steps does the Step Pyramid have?
2. What type of tombs did pyramids grow out of?
3. Who was buried inside the Step Pyramid?
4. Who was the architect of the Step Pyramid?

Answers:
1. Six 2. Mastaba tombs 3. King Djoser 4. Imhotep

5 **The architect Imhotep built the Step Pyramid.**
He was Djoser's vizier, or chief minister, and was in charge of all building projects. It was his idea to build Djoser's tomb from stone, and to create a pyramid. Imhotep was also a poet, a priest, and a doctor. Many years after his death he was made into a god, responsible for wisdom, writing and medicine.

6 **The Step Pyramid is at Saqarra – an ancient Egyptian cemetery.**
The pyramid was built around 2650 BCE. It is about 200 feet high and its sides are more than 325 feet in length. King Djoser was buried inside one of the chambers that were carved into the solid rock beneath the pyramid.

The Step Pyramid was a series of platforms on top of each other. It was an experiment in building a tall structure, and it led the way to true pyramids with smooth sides.

Sneferu, the pyramid king

7 Kings who came after Djoser also wanted to be buried in pyramids. King Sneferu (2613–2589 BCE) had a step pyramid built at Meidum rising to 300 feet in height. Later his builders added an outer layer of stone, to create a smooth-sided pyramid. Then, for some unknown reason, the pyramid was abandoned. The stone was stripped away, probably for other buildings, leaving a tower surrounded by rubble.

The pyramid at Meidum is an odd shape because it has lost its outer layer of stone. Some experts think the pyramid may have been started before Sneferu's reign.

I DON'T BELIEVE IT!

If you could talk to an ancient Egyptian, he wouldn't know what a pyramid was! In his language a pyramid was a "mr" (say: "mer"), and pyramids were "mrw" (say: "meroo").

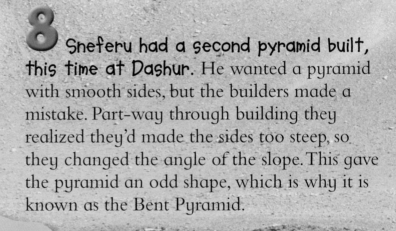

8 Sneferu had a second pyramid built, this time at Dashur. He wanted a pyramid with smooth sides, but the builders made a mistake. Part-way through building they realized they'd made the sides too steep, so they changed the angle of the slope. This gave the pyramid an odd shape, which is why it is known as the Bent Pyramid.

9 The Bent Pyramid is more than 344 feet high, but it would have been at least 100 feet taller if the angle of the sides hadn't been changed. It is an unusual pyramid as it has two entrances and two burial chambers. Both of these burial chambers are now empty.

King Sneferu's workers began building the Bent Pyramid in about 2600 BCE. It has more of its fine stone facing left than any other pyramid.

10 Sneferu was the "pyramid king" who learned from his mistakes. The Bent Pyramid wasn't good enough for him, so he planned another pyramid, also at Dashur. This is the Red Pyramid (also known as the North Pyramid). The builders got the angle right this time, and the sides slope gently to a point. It was the first "true" pyramid.

The Red Pyramid was the third and last pyramid built by King Sneferu. He was probably buried in this pyramid in about 2589 BCE.

11 Sneferu's Red Pyramid is 341 feet high, and its sides are 722 feet long. Today, it is named for the red limestone it is built from, but when it was finished it would have actually been white. This is because the sides were finished with slabs of gleaming, white limestone. A passage leads inside the pyramid to three chambers.

12 **Egypt's most famous pyramids are at Giza.** In ancient Egyptian times a burial ground was known as 'kher neter', meaning 'the necropolis'. Giza was a necropolis and this was where three of ancient Egypt's most famous kings were buried in pyramids.

The Giza pyramids. From left to right they are the pyramids of Menkaure, Khafre and Khufu.

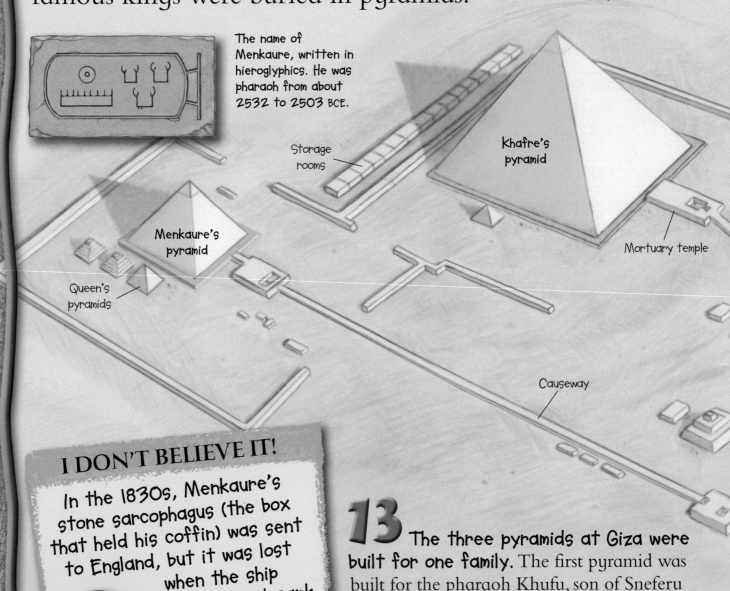

The name of Menkaure, written in hieroglyphics. He was pharaoh from about 2532 to 2503 BCE.

Storage rooms

Khafre's pyramid

Mortuary temple

Menkaure's pyramid

Queen's pyramids

Causeway

I DON'T BELIEVE IT!

In the 1830s, Menkaure's stone sarcophagus (the box that held his coffin) was sent to England, but it was lost when the ship carrying it sank off the coast of Spain.

13 **The three pyramids at Giza were built for one family.** The first pyramid was built for the pharaoh Khufu, son of Sneferu (who built the first 'true' pyramid). The second pyramid was for Khafre, Khufu's son. Last of all came the pyramid for Menkaure, son of Khafre, grandson of Khufu.

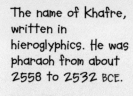

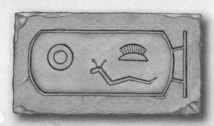

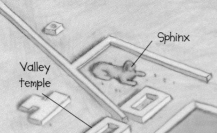

Mastabas of Khufu's officials

Khufu's pyramid

Queen's pyramids

Mastabas of Khufu's relatives

Sphinx

Valley temple

15 Khafre's pyramid is 470 feet high.

It is shorter than Khufu's pyramid but looks bigger as it was built on slightly higher ground. All three pyramids were originally covered by a layer of white limestone. Only Khafre's pyramid still has some of its limestone blocks in place, right at the very top. The pyramid is guarded by a famous statue called the Sphinx.

The name of Khufu, written in hieroglyphics. He was pharaoh from about 2589 to 2566 BCE.

16 The smallest Giza pyramid was built for Menkaure.

It is only 213 feet high – less than half the height of Khufu's and Khafre's pyramids. Another difference is in its building materials. When its sides were finished, only the top two-thirds were covered with slabs of expensive white limestone. The bottom third was covered with cheaper blocks of granite, some of which are still in place today.

14 Khufu's pyramid is known as the Great Pyramid.

It is the finest of all the Egyptian pyramids, and is about 4500 years old. It is the largest Egyptian pyramid ever built, rising almost 500 feet into the sky. Inside are passages, shafts and chambers. Khufu was buried in a central chamber of the pyramid.

Why build pyramids?

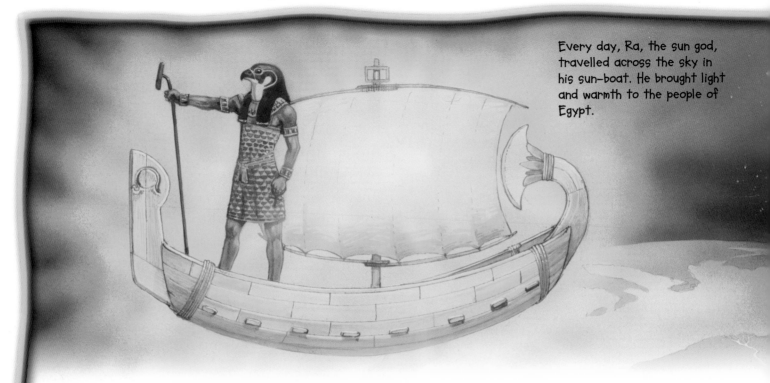

Every day, Ra, the sun god, travelled across the sky in his sun–boat. He brought light and warmth to the people of Egypt.

17 **The ancient Egyptians believed in many different gods.** The most important was Ra, the sun god, who was said to be the very first pharaoh. Pharaohs who ruled Egypt after Ra were thought of as representatives of the gods. They were god-like kings, who had come to Egypt in human form to do the gods' work.

After a person died, their personality left their body. The ancient Egyptians called it the Ba and thought it looked like a bird with a human head. The Ba made the dangerous journey to the underworld, where the dead were judged.

18 **One purpose of a pyramid was to be a tomb for a dead pharaoh.** It was where his body was buried, and where it was meant to forever rest in peace. His pyramid was also a storehouse, and was filled with all the food, personal belongings, gifts and magical spells he would need in the afterlife.

19 In the 1990s, Robert Bauval and Adrian Gilbert wrote *The Orion Mystery*. They pointed out that the Giza pyramids match the arrangement of the three main stars in the "belt" of the Orion constellation (a pattern of stars). However, when the pyramids were built the stars in Orion's belt were in different positions in relation to the Earth – so the Egyptians could not have used the stars to help them work out where to place the pyramids!

I DON'T BELIEVE IT!

Pyramids were built with narrow shafts that pointed to the stars. The Egyptians believed that the pharaoh's soul used these to travel between the world of the living and the afterlife.

20 A pyramid was a "living link" between the dead pharaoh and his country. Everyone in ancient Egypt knew that a pyramid was the last resting place of one of their kings, and as long as the pyramid was there, the pharaoh was there, too. While he was alive, it was a pharaoh's job to protect his people and his country. Once he died, a pyramid acted as a constant reminder of the role the pharaoh had played in people's lives.

Orion's constellation is shown by the diagram on the left. The constellation is in the shape of a hunter with a bow. The three stars in the center of the hunter's body form Orion's belt, and the image above shows how they appear in the night sky.

Building a pyramid

21 The ancient Egyptians built their pyramids on the west bank of the river Nile. This was because the Egyptians linked the west with death, as this was where the sun set. The site had to be far enough away from the river to avoid flooding, but close enough for building materials to be transported to it.

Builders made slots in the bedrock that were filled with water. The water was at the same level in every slot, showing the builders how much rock to remove in order to make the site flat.

22 After a site was chosen, the position of the pyramid was decided. Egyptian pyramids have sides that face north, south, east and west, but it is not clear how this was worked out. People may have used the stars to work out the position of north. Once they knew where north was, it was easy to work out the positions of south, east and west.

23 The site had to be flat, so the pyramid would rise straight up. One idea is that the builders flooded the site with water, and measured down from the surface. By keeping the measurement the same across the site, it showed them how much bedrock had to be cut away to make the site level.

At the stone quarries, teams of men had specific jobs to do. Some split and levered rough blocks away from the bedrock. Others smoothed the sides of the blocks, and then they were ready to transport to the building site.

24 Pyramid workers used simple tools.
Mattocks (digging tools) were used to clear the building site, and the rubble was carried away in woven reed baskets. In the stone quarries, stone was cut using mauls (stone hammers), copper chisels, and wedges. Woodworkers cut and shaped wood using copper saws and chisels, drills, hammers, and planes.

25 Hundreds of men usually worked in the stone quarries.
At busy times there may have been a few thousand. They worked in teams, cutting blocks of limestone and granite. The bedrock was marked with the outlines of blocks, and then the outlines were chiselled away to leave a grid of grooves. Copper wedges were knocked into the grooves to make the bedrock split. Last of all, wooden levers pried the blocks free.

Raising the blocks

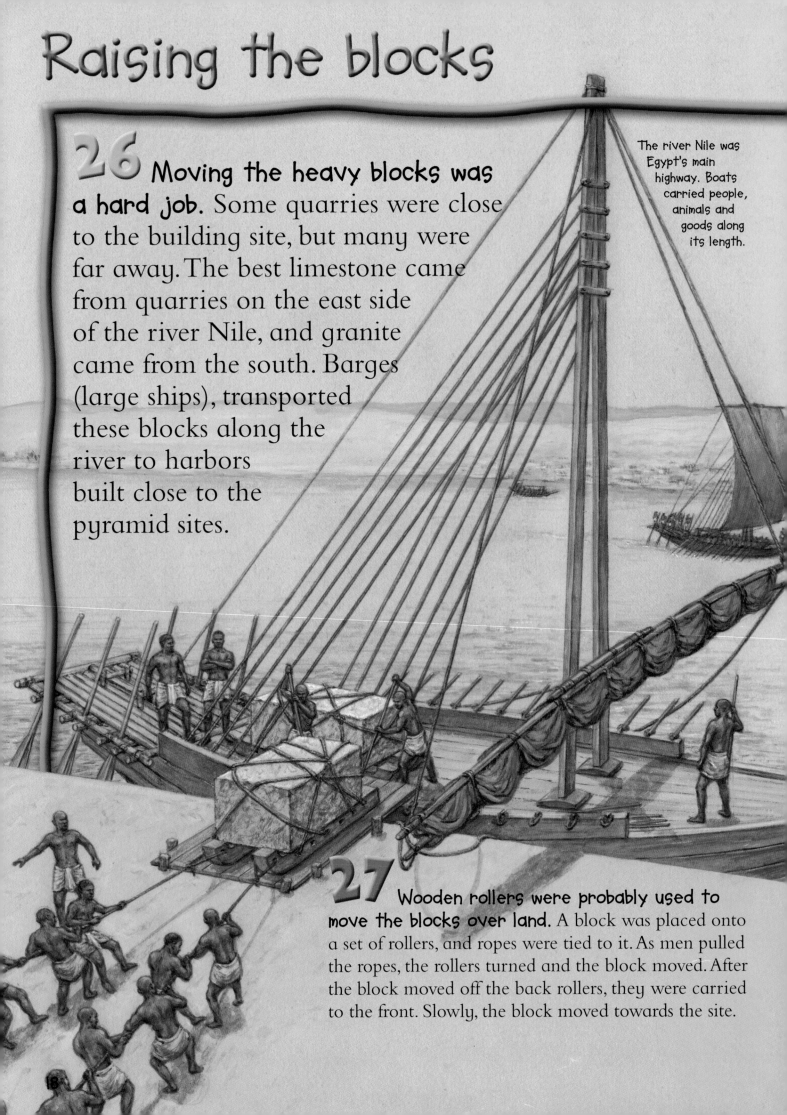

26 **Moving the heavy blocks was a hard job.** Some quarries were close to the building site, but many were far away. The best limestone came from quarries on the east side of the river Nile, and granite came from the south. Barges (large ships), transported these blocks along the river to harbors built close to the pyramid sites.

The river Nile was Egypt's main highway. Boats carried people, animals and goods along its length.

27 **Wooden rollers were probably used to move the blocks over land.** A block was placed onto a set of rollers, and ropes were tied to it. As men pulled the ropes, the rollers turned and the block moved. After the block moved off the back rollers, they were carried to the front. Slowly, the block moved towards the site.

28 How the blocks reached their final destination is a puzzle. Historians agree that they were dragged up ramps made from hard soil and rubble – but there's disagreement about what shape the ramps were. One idea says there was one ramp that wrapped around the growing pyramid in a spiral shape. Another says there was a straight ramp against one side of the pyramid. A third idea is that there were four ramps, one on each side of the pyramid.

Pharaohs probably inspected their pyramids as they were built. Their crowns showed which part of Egypt they ruled – the White Crown represented Upper Egypt, whereas the Red Crown represented Lower Egypt.

29 Once a block had been moved up the ramp, it was set in place. This was skilled work, and the stone setters had to make sure the blocks fitted neatly together. They used wooden levers to move the blocks around, and by the time one block was in place, another one had been brought up the ramp to be fitted. It was non-stop work.

30 Stonemasons built the chambers and passages inside the pyramid. Outside, the last block was put in place. This was the capstone, or pyramidion, a pyramid-shaped block that went at the top. It was covered in a thin layer of gold, which shone brightly in the sunlight.

31 Finally, the ramps were removed. As the ramps came down, workers set slabs of limestone in place. These gave the sides a smooth finish. Inside, painters decorated the burial chamber walls and ceilings with pictures and magical spells. The pyramid was finished, and was ready to be used as a pharaoh's tomb.

ANCIENT ART

Use books and the Internet to find pictures of the beautiful paintings that the Egyptians created on the walls of burial chambers. You could even try to paint some of your own!

Pyramid people

32 Building a pyramid was a huge project. It needed planning, and a large workforce. An architect was in charge of the whole project. He updated the pharaoh with its progress, and instructed the workers.

33 Historians used to think that the pyramids of ancient Egypt were built by slaves. Many historians now believe that slaves did not build the pyramids, but that instead, they were built by hard-working, ordinary men who came from villages across Egypt.

The pyramid builders lived in small towns near the pyramids on the west "dead" side of the river Nile, where people did not usually live.

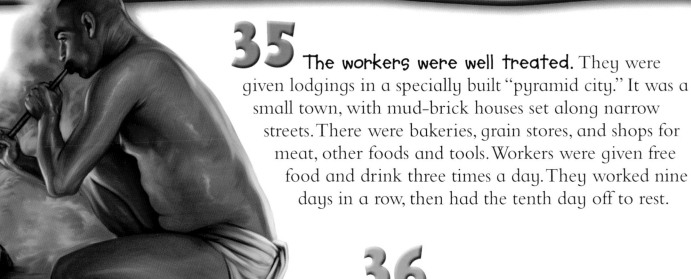

35 **The workers were well treated.** They were given lodgings in a specially built "pyramid city." It was a small town, with mud-brick houses set along narrow streets. There were bakeries, grain stores, and shops for meat, other foods and tools. Workers were given free food and drink three times a day. They worked nine days in a row, then had the tenth day off to rest.

Metal-workers blew through tubes to increase the heat of a fire until it was hot enough to melt copper ore. Copper was used to make tools.

36 **The workforce was split into two big teams of around 1000 men.** The teams that built the pyramid of Menkaure were called "Friends of Menkaure" and "Drunkards of Menkaure." Each team was split into five smaller teams of 200 men, who were called the "Great," the "Asiatic," the "Green," the "Little," and the "Last." In turn, these teams were made up of 20 groups of ten men.

34 **Building a pyramid was dangerous work, and accidents happened.** The skeletons of pyramid builders show that they suffered from broken and crushed bones, and from worn out joints. In many cases workers' broken bones healed, but if an arm or leg was badly crushed, it was amputated (cut off). Worn joints could not be repaired, so workers had to live with the pain.

This wall painting from a tomb shows workers shaping pieces of wood and making mud-bricks.

The Great Pyramid

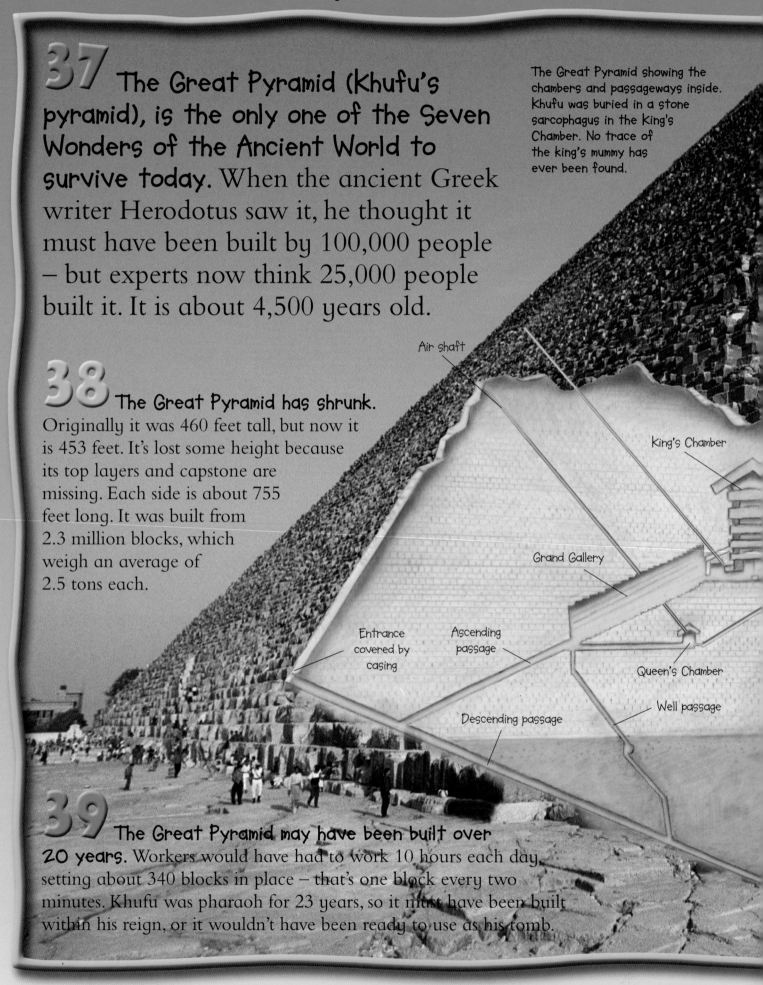

37 **The Great Pyramid (Khufu's pyramid), is the only one of the Seven Wonders of the Ancient World to survive today.** When the ancient Greek writer Herodotus saw it, he thought it must have been built by 100,000 people – but experts now think 25,000 people built it. It is about 4,500 years old.

The Great Pyramid showing the chambers and passageways inside. Khufu was buried in a stone sarcophagus in the King's Chamber. No trace of the king's mummy has ever been found.

38 **The Great Pyramid has shrunk.** Originally it was 460 feet tall, but now it is 453 feet. It's lost some height because its top layers and capstone are missing. Each side is about 755 feet long. It was built from 2.3 million blocks, which weigh an average of 2.5 tons each.

Air shaft

King's Chamber

Grand Gallery

Entrance covered by casing

Ascending passage

Queen's Chamber

Well passage

Descending passage

39 **The Great Pyramid may have been built over 20 years.** Workers would have had to work 10 hours each day, setting about 340 blocks in place – that's one block every two minutes. Khufu was pharaoh for 23 years, so it must have been built within his reign, or it wouldn't have been ready to use as his tomb.

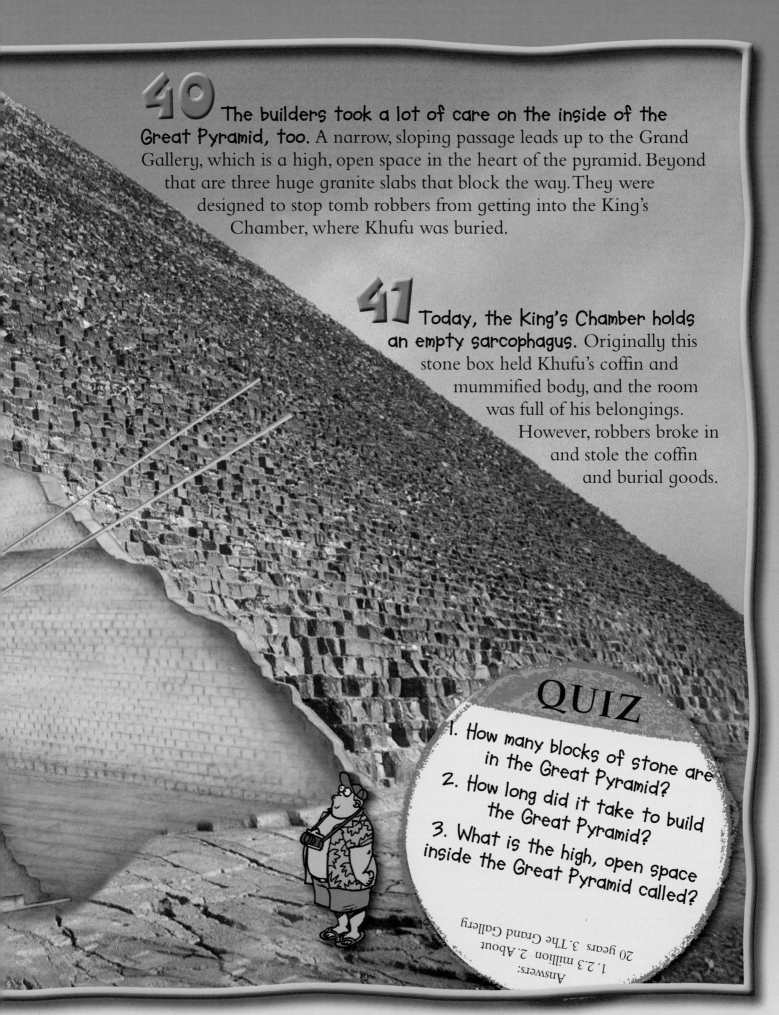

40 **The builders took a lot of care on the inside of the Great Pyramid, too.** A narrow, sloping passage leads up to the Grand Gallery, which is a high, open space in the heart of the pyramid. Beyond that are three huge granite slabs that block the way. They were designed to stop tomb robbers from getting into the King's Chamber, where Khufu was buried.

41 **Today, the King's Chamber holds an empty sarcophagus.** Originally this stone box held Khufu's coffin and mummified body, and the room was full of his belongings. However, robbers broke in and stole the coffin and burial goods.

QUIZ

1. How many blocks of stone are in the Great Pyramid?
2. How long did it take to build the Great Pyramid?
3. What is the high, open space inside the Great Pyramid called?

Answers:
1. 2.3 million 2. About 20 years 3. The Grand Gallery

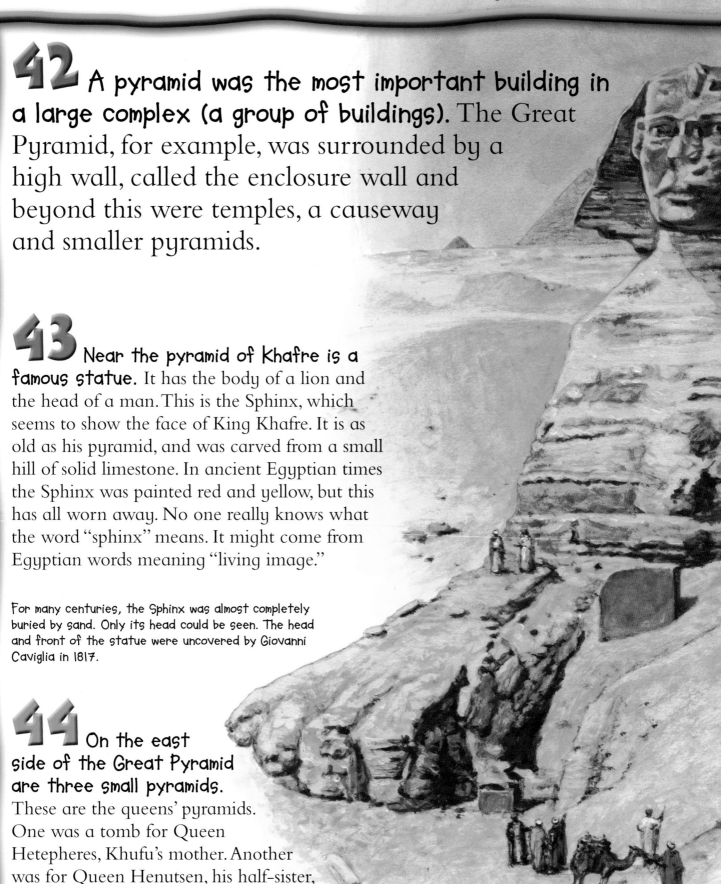

Around the Great Pyramid

42 **A pyramid was the most important building in a large complex (a group of buildings).** The Great Pyramid, for example, was surrounded by a high wall, called the enclosure wall and beyond this were temples, a causeway and smaller pyramids.

43 **Near the pyramid of Khafre is a famous statue.** It has the body of a lion and the head of a man. This is the Sphinx, which seems to show the face of King Khafre. It is as old as his pyramid, and was carved from a small hill of solid limestone. In ancient Egyptian times the Sphinx was painted red and yellow, but this has all worn away. No one really knows what the word "sphinx" means. It might come from Egyptian words meaning "living image."

For many centuries, the Sphinx was almost completely buried by sand. Only its head could be seen. The head and front of the statue were uncovered by Giovanni Caviglia in 1817.

44 **On the east side of the Great Pyramid are three small pyramids.** These are the queens' pyramids. One was a tomb for Queen Hetepheres, Khufu's mother. Another was for Queen Henutsen, his half-sister, and the third may have been for Queen Meritetis, about whom little is known.

45 A fourth pyramid stood near the Great Pyramid. It was small, and only its base remains today. Khufu may have used it as a changing room when he took part in the sed festival, during which he told the gods that he had done all they had asked.

This is one of the boats found buried at the foot of the Great Pyramid. All the pieces were put back together, and the boat is now in a museum.

46 When archaeologists dug along the south side of the Great Pyramid, they found two boat-shaped pits. They opened one, and out came a jumble of 1224 pieces of wood. It took years to join the pieces together, but eventually a boat measuring 141 feet in length was rebuilt. It may have been used to transport the king's mummy to the pyramid.

I DON'T BELIEVE IT!

Outside the Great Pyramid archaeologists found two pits. The first contained a boat. The second pit has not been opened but a tiny camera has been sent inside — its photos show another boat!

Resting in peace

47 **After a pharaoh died, his body was mummified.** This stopped it from rotting. The ancient Egyptians mummified their dead because they believed a person could only have a life after death if their body was preserved. It took 70 days to mummify a body and it was then ready to be buried.

48 **Once the mummy was ready, it could be buried in its pyramid tomb.** It was pulled over land on a sled, then taken by boat across the river Nile. There were many mourners – some were relatives, others were professional mourners who beat their chests, pulled their hair, and wailed aloud. Priests sprinkled milk on the ground, and burned incense.

49 **When the procession reached the pyramid complex, sacred rites were performed.** The mummy was taken from temple to temple, until it entered the burial chamber. It was then taken from its coffin and a priest touched its mouth, eyes, ears and nose with a Y-shaped stone. This was the Opening of the Mouth ceremony, and was believed to restore the pharaoh's ability to breathe, see and hear.

The mummified body of an Egyptian pharaoh was transported across the river Nile to the west bank – the side of the river where his pyramid tomb had been built for him.

50 The priests placed the mummy back inside its coffin, which was put into a stone sarcophagus. Grave goods were stacked inside the burial chamber for the pharaoh to use in the next life. These included clothes, furniture, food, and hundreds of everyday items. Then the priests left, and workers sealed the tomb so that no one would be able to get inside (or so they hoped).

51 After the pyramid was sealed, the pharaoh was believed to travel to the afterlife. On the way he met 42 judges, who accused him of crimes. He denied them all. After this, his heart was weighed against a feather, to see if he had lead a good and truthful life. If he had, the scales balanced, and he was allowed to enter the afterlife.

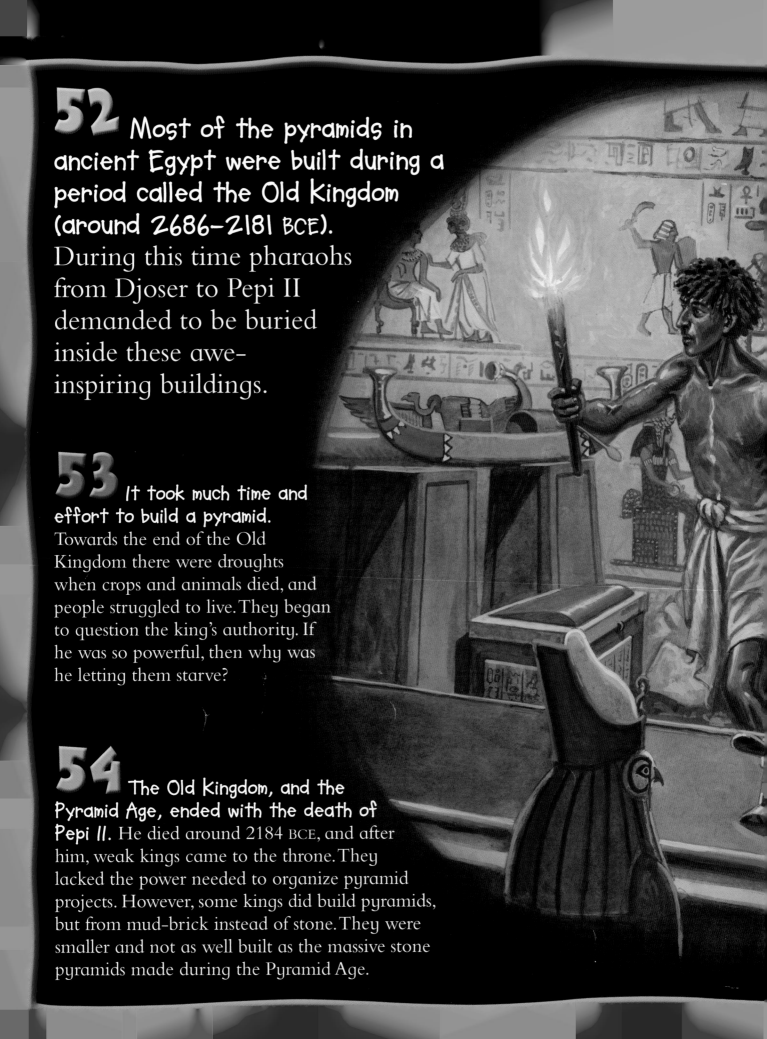

52 Most of the pyramids in ancient Egypt were built during a period called the Old Kingdom (around 2686–2181 BCE). During this time pharaohs from Djoser to Pepi II demanded to be buried inside these awe-inspiring buildings.

53 It took much time and effort to build a pyramid. Towards the end of the Old Kingdom there were droughts when crops and animals died, and people struggled to live. They began to question the king's authority. If he was so powerful, then why was he letting them starve?

54 The Old Kingdom, and the Pyramid Age, ended with the death of Pepi II. He died around 2184 BCE, and after him, weak kings came to the throne. They lacked the power needed to organize pyramid projects. However, some kings did build pyramids, but from mud-brick instead of stone. They were smaller and not as well built as the massive stone pyramids made during the Pyramid Age.

55 Pyramids were supposed to be sealed forever – but every one of them was broken into. For tomb robbers, pyramids were very tempting places. It was impossible to hide a pyramid, so robbers knew exactly where to look. Despite all the blocked passageways and hidden entrances, thieves got in and stole the contents. If a robber was caught, he was put to death, usually by impaling on a sharp wooden stake.

Even small objects such as amulets (lucky charms) were taken by tomb robbers. This is a scarab charm made of green jasper, taken from the tomb of the pharaoh Sobekemsat.

56 The last thing the kings of ancient Egypt wanted was for their tombs to be broken into. Pyramids weren't perfect resting places after all, and for this reason a new type of tomb was needed. Pharaohs of the New Kingdom (around 1550 to 1070 BCE) were buried in tombs cut into the side of a remote valley instead. It's called the Valley of the Kings.

Tomb robbers made their living from breaking into tombs and stealing the contents. It was a family business, passed on from father to son. Robbers took great risks, as they faced death if caught.

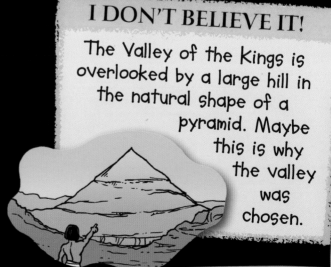

I DON'T BELIEVE IT!

The Valley of the Kings is overlooked by a large hill in the natural shape of a pyramid. Maybe this is why the valley was chosen.

Egypt's last pyramids

57 Deir el-Medineh was a village built to house the workers building tombs in the Valley of the Kings. Their kings were buried out of sight in underground tombs, but some workers were buried in tombs with small pyramids above them.

58 The small pyramids at Deir el-Medineh were ordinary people's private tombs. They were built of mud-brick, which was cheap and easy to make. The outside of the pyramid was covered with plaster to give a smooth finish, and pictures were painted on the inside walls.

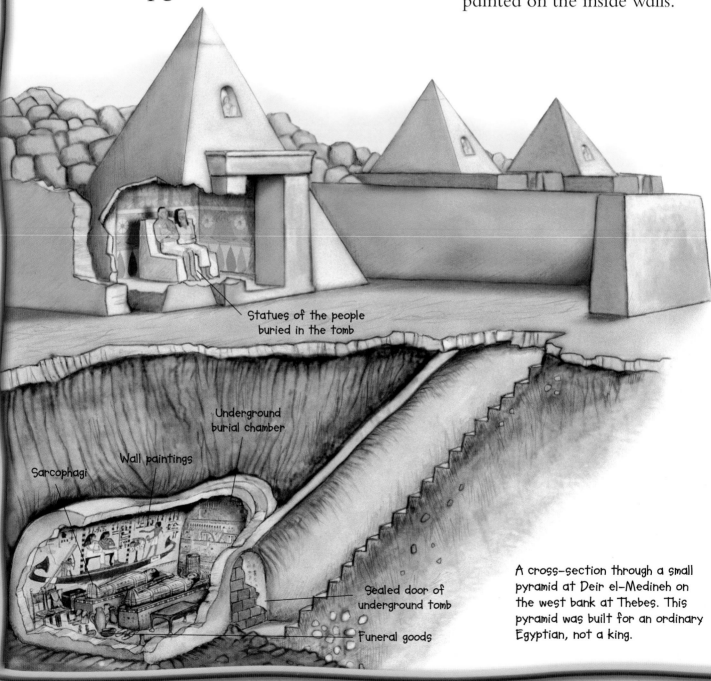

Statues of the people buried in the tomb

Underground burial chamber

Wall paintings

Sarcophagi

Sealed door of underground tomb

Funeral goods

A cross-section through a small pyramid at Deir el-Medineh on the west bank at Thebes. This pyramid was built for an ordinary Egyptian, not a king.

59 Mud-brick was the basic building material in ancient Egypt. Brick-makers collected mud, water and straw, then mixed them by treading them together. This mixture was pressed into brick-shaped wooden frames. The bricks were removed from the frames and left to bake in the sun. They were light and easy to build with.

60 From 770 BCE, around 180 small pyramids were built in Nubia, at Meroe. They were built by kings and nobles to be used as tombs. Perhaps Nubian kings wanted to use pyramids to show their royal power.

61 The Nubian pyramids were small and short, had steep sides, and were very pointed. Most were built from sandstone. The last pyramids were built at Meroe, around 350 CE when Nubia was conquered by the Axumites. This was the end of 3000 years of pyramid-building in ancient Egypt.

The pyramids at Meroe are in varying states of disrepair due to people breaking into them looking for treasure, as well as stealing the stone blocks.

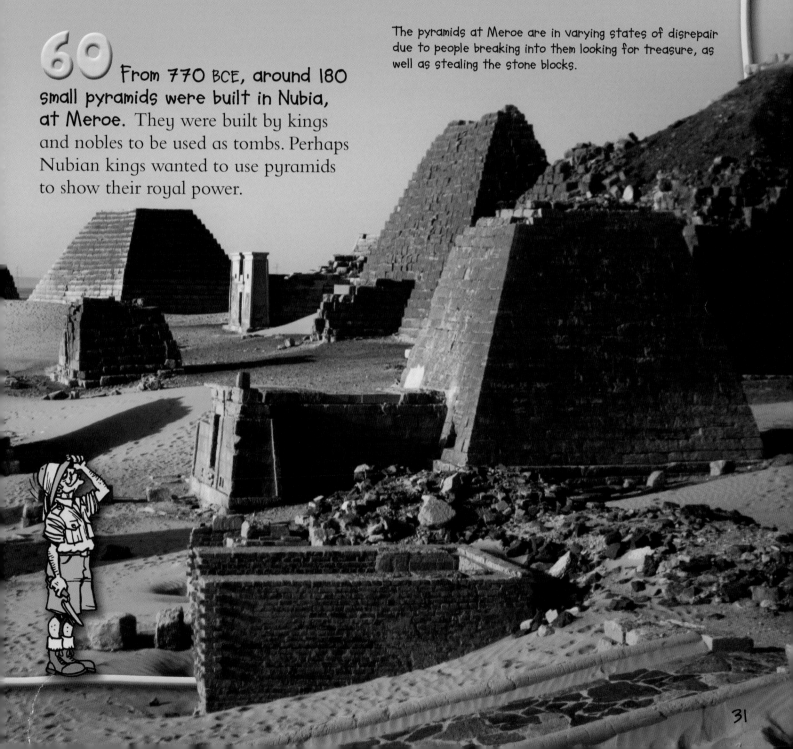

Ziggurats

62 The people of Mesopotamia built pyramid-shaped buildings called ziggurats. Mesopotamia was the ancient name for the land between the rivers Euphrates and Tigris, in what is now Iraq. The name ziggurat comes from the ancient word 'ziqquratu', meaning 'mountain top'.

A ziggurat, or temple tower, in a town in ancient Mesopotamia (Iraq). A priest, wearing a fish costume, leads a procession of worshippers to the temple at the top of the ziggurat.

63 The first ziggurats were built around 2100 BCE at the city of Ur, Mesopotamia. This was roughly the same time that the Egyptian pyramids were built, but the buildings were very different. A pyramid was a pointed tomb with smooth sides, a ziggurat was a tower with a temple, built on a series of platforms.

Tower

Temple

Priest

Procession of worshippers

QUIZ

1. What was at the top of a ziggurat?
2. In which city was the Tower of Babel?
3. True or false: a ziggurat had smooth sides.
4. What were ziggurats made from?

Answers:
1. A temple 2. Babylon
3. False – a ziggurat had stepped sides
4. Mud-brick

64 Ziggurats were the center of religious life in Mesopotamian cities. There was a constant bustle of priests, officials and worshippers. The faithful believed ziggurats were links between heaven and earth. As they climbed up to the temple they felt that they were getting closer to the gods.

65 A ziggurat was made from several flat platforms, built on top of each other. These were reached by ramps and outer staircases. The building was made from mud-bricks, held together by wooden beams and reed matting. Some outer bricks were coated in bright colors.

66 The largest ziggurat was in the city of Babylon. It was built around 600 BCE by King Nebuchadnezzar II. At this time it was called 'Etemenanki', which means 'house of the foundation of heaven on earth'. It had seven platforms, and was 328 feet tall. The Book of Genesis, in the Bible, calls Babylon 'Babel', and refers to a tall brick tower 'that reaches to the heavens'. This probably refers to the ziggurat, which became known as the Tower of Babel.

Pyramids of the Maya

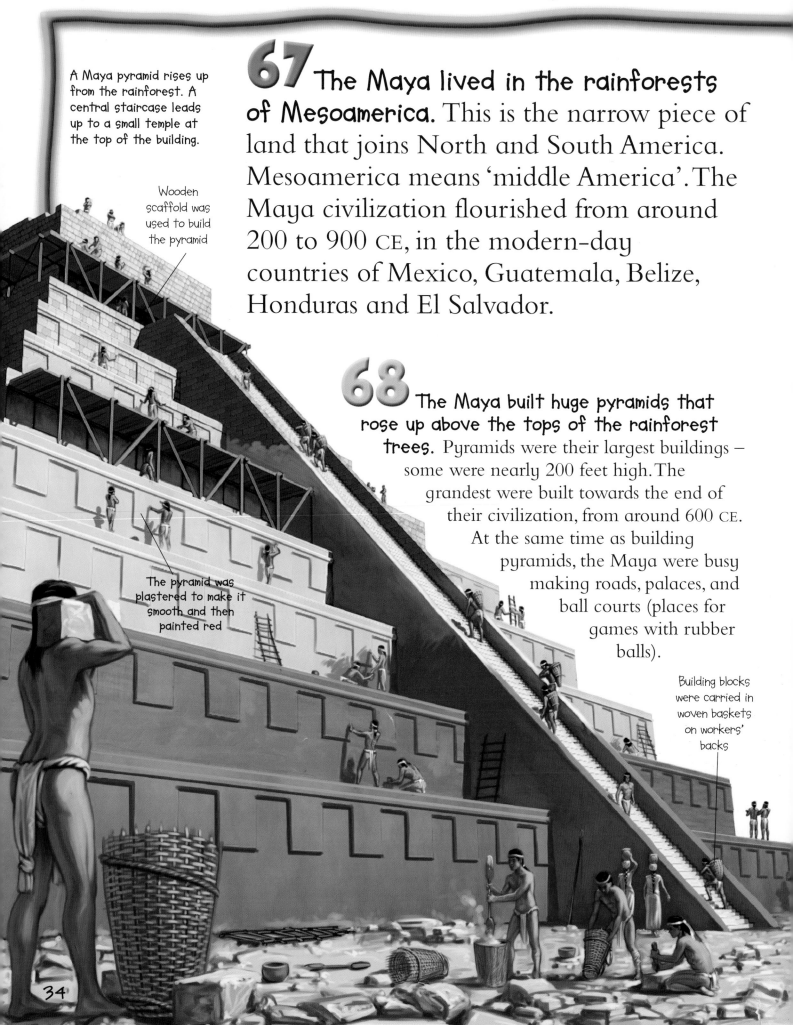

A Maya pyramid rises up from the rainforest. A central staircase leads up to a small temple at the top of the building.

Wooden scaffold was used to build the pyramid

The pyramid was plastered to make it smooth and then painted red

67 **The Maya lived in the rainforests of Mesoamerica.** This is the narrow piece of land that joins North and South America. Mesoamerica means 'middle America'. The Maya civilization flourished from around 200 to 900 CE, in the modern-day countries of Mexico, Guatemala, Belize, Honduras and El Salvador.

68 **The Maya built huge pyramids that rose up above the tops of the rainforest trees.** Pyramids were their largest buildings – some were nearly 200 feet high. The grandest were built towards the end of their civilization, from around 600 CE. At the same time as building pyramids, the Maya were busy making roads, palaces, and ball courts (places for games with rubber balls).

Building blocks were carried in woven baskets on workers' backs

69 Maya pyramids were not made of solid stone. They were pyramid-shaped mounds of compacted earth and rubble, with stone walls on the outside. The walls were built to form a series of steps. Then they were layered with plaster to make them smooth, and painted red. A temple was built on the top, reached by one or more staircases at the front of the building.

The Temple of the Inscriptions is the tomb of Pacal the Great. It is 75 feet high.

Some Maya pyramids had images of human skulls carved all around them. They represented the skulls of enemies defeated in battle.

71 The Temple of the Inscriptions at Palenque, Mexico, is the most famous of all Maya pyramids. It was built around 680 CE, as a tomb for the Maya king Pacal. His tomb was found after archaeologists lifted a stone slab at the top of the pyramid and climbed down a passage. Pacal was buried inside a huge stone sarcophagus. Its carved lid shows the king on his way to the afterlife.

70 Maya pyramids were temples to the gods and tombs for dead kings. During religious ceremonies, priests climbed the steep staircases. They believed the higher they climbed, the nearer they came to their gods. In the temple at the top, prisoners were sacrificed as offerings to the gods. Crowds gathered in courtyards around the pyramid to watch the blood flow.

I DON'T BELIEVE IT!
Pacal was buried with a mask of jade (a hard green stone) covering his face. The mask was stolen from a museum by two students in 1985. Police tracked it down in 1989, and returned it to the museum.

Pyramids of Mexico

72 Many pyramids were built by the ancient peoples of Mexico, such as the Olmecs, the Toltecs, and the Aztecs. Some of the oldest and largest are at Teotihuacan. One of the best known is the Pyramid of the Magician, at Uxmal.

73 Long ago, a city called Teotihuacan existed in Mexico. Around 500 CE, it was one of the world's largest cities. In the city centre were two huge pyramids – the Pyramid of the Moon and the Pyramid of the Sun.

The Pyramid of the Magician was built by the Maya. They began building it in the 500s CE, and it was in use for about 400 years. It is unusual because it has curved sides, and is an oval shape.

I DON'T BELIEVE IT!

Around 500 CE, so many people lived in Teotihuacan, that it was one of the biggest cities in the world!

The Pyramid of the Sun is made from around 2.5 million tonnes of earth and stone.

76 The city of Tula also became important after the fall of Teotihuacan. It was the capital of the Toltecs, who built several temple-pyramids there. At the top of Pyramid B are columns carved decoratively to look like warriors, which supported the temple roof. When the Toltecs lost power, a new group became important in Mexico – the Aztecs.

74 The Pyramid of the Sun, Teotihuacan, was built around 2000 years ago. According to Mexican legend, it was built at the place where time began. Archaeologists discovered a small shrine built over a sacred cave at the site. Over time the shrine was made bigger, and became a series of platforms rising to 250 feet in height. At the top was a temple. The whole pyramid was covered with painted plaster.

The warrior columns at the top of the Toltec pyramid at Tula are 15 feet high.

75 The city of Teotihuacan was abandoned around 750 CE. No one really knows why, but its pyramids were burned, statues were broken, and the people left. After the fall of Teotihuacan, other cities rose to power. In the city of Cholula, a huge pyramid-shaped temple was built. The Great Pyramid of Cholula is the largest pyramid in the Americas. Its sides are 1,476 feet in length, and it is about 216 feet in height.

Pyramids of the Aztecs

77 The Aztecs lived in Mexico from around 1325 CE to 1521 CE. Their capital city, Tenochtitlan, was built on an island in the middle of Lake Texcoco. Today, the lake has been drained, and Mexico City has been built over the Aztec capital's ruins. Beneath the modern streets are the remains of a giant Aztec pyramid.

78 Aztec pyramids were built as temples, where sacrifices were made to the gods. They were the main town buildings, and were surrounded by public squares. The squares were viewing places, where the public gathered to watch priests at work at the top of the pyramid.

79 Aztecs sacrificed animals and humans to their gods to ensure that the universe would continue to exist. Every town had sacrificial ceremonies. Many prisoners who were captured in battle slowly walked towards the place of execution. The victims' hearts, limbs, and even heads were removed during ceremonies.

An Aztec knife with a stone blade and decorated mosaic handle. It may have been used to sacrifice victims.

80 The Aztec pyramid at Tenochtitlan was built over roughly 200 years. It reached its final shape around 1519. At 98 feet high, it was made from gravel and mud. The outside was faced with stone and brightly painted plaster. Twin staircases led to the top, where there were a pair of shrines to the city's gods of rain and war. When the Aztec empire was conquered by Spain in 1521, the pyramid became known as the "Templo Mayor" (Great

A reconstruction of the Aztec temples and squares at Tenochtitlan, present-day Mexico City.

Shrine to the god of war

Shrine to the god of rain

Templo Mayor

Public square

The Aztecs sacrificed human victims at shrines built at the top of their pyramids.

MAKE A MOSAIC

You will need:
colored paper cut into small squares •
plain paper • a pencil • glue

1. Draw a design onto the plain paper using the pencil.
2. Fill in your design with different colored squares of paper and stick them down with glue.

Now you have your very own mosaic!

81 The Spanish killed many Aztecs, and destroyed the Great Temple. They believed that human sacrifice was wrong, and that the Aztec religion was false. Some of the stone was used for new buildings, such as the Metropolitan Cathedral, in Mexico City. The pyramid was reduced to a low mound, and became known as the "Hill of the Dogs" because stray dogs lived there. By chance, in 1978, workmen discovered the pyramid's ruins and, archaeologists began excavating them.

82 Pyramids have always attracted visitors. Robbers, archaeologists, tourists and film-makers have all flocked to them. An early visitor to Egypt's Great Pyramid was Abdullah al-Mamun of Baghdad, in modern Iraq. His men tunnelled into the pyramid in about 820 CE searching for treasure.

Ancient Egypt's secrets are being uncovered today by archaeologists using a variety of delicate techniques. Here, a team is working close to the Step Pyramid.

83 The first major excavations of the Giza pyramids began in the 19th century. Giovanni Caviglia removed the sand that covered the Sphinx, and Howard Vyse used dynamite to blast into the pyramids, even blowing a chunk off the Sphinx!

84 The Giza pyramids were studied throughout the 20th century. In the 1990s, people working for a television series called *NOVA* built a small pyramid using processes and materials similar to the Egyptians. This experiment hoped to answer questions about how pyramids were built.

I DON'T BELIEVE IT!

Napoleon worked out that the three pyramids at Giza contained enough stone to build a wall around France an inch wide and a foot high!

85 Pyramids have always been looted, and those of the Americas are still under threat. Peoples such as the Incas, Nasca and Moche built pyramids here. The Moche lived along the northern coast of what is now Peru, from 100 BCE to 650 CE. In 1987 robbers dug into a Moche pyramid at Sipan, Peru. Inside, a king lay surrounded by gold and precious stones. Before the robbers did too much damage, archaeologists were able to excavate it properly.

The Lord of Sipan, Peru, was buried with many valuable items, and with servants to look after him in the afterlife.

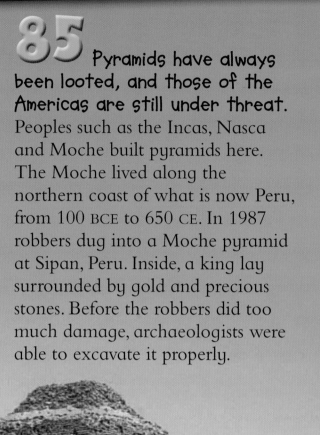

86 Archaeologists are using new technologies to learn more about pyramids. In 2002, archaeologists wanted to explore a narrow shaft leading from an unfinished chamber in the Great Pyramid. They thought a secret burial chamber could exist behind the stone panel that blocks the shaft. So they created a special robot to drill through the panel. Unfortunately, the robot only revealed an empty space leading to another panel!

A world of pyramids

87 The Romans were experts at copying other people's ideas. For example, in their capital at Rome, Italy, is the Pyramid of Cestius. The Romans ruled Egypt between 30 BCE and 395 CE, and the Egyptian pyramids had impressed them. The Roman pyramid was built about 12 BCE, as a tomb for Gaius Cestius, a Roman politician.

88 There are ancient pyramids in China, but little is known about them. Near the city of Xian are about 100 pyramid-shaped mounds made from soil. Some are quite low, but a few rise up to 200 feet. These are the burial mounds of China's early emperors and empresses, built between 200 BCE and 800 CE.

The Pyramid of Cestius, Rome, is made from concrete covered with slabs of white marble. It is about 118 feet high.

The temple of Borobudur, Java, was built in the 800s CE. It is decorated with 504 statues of Buddha.

89 The ancient Buddhist temple of Borobudur, on the island of Java, looks like a step pyramid. The different levels reflect the ideas of Buddhist faith, and the temple is used as a center of religious practice. There are several temples at Bagan, Myanmar (Burma), which have tall spires that look like narrow, pointed pyramids.

90 During the 19th century, there were even plans to have a pyramid built in London! At this time cemeteries were filling up and people were worried there was not enough space. So they came up with a plan to build a giant pyramid on Primrose Hill, to hold the bodies of five million Londoners. It was never actually built.

Pyramid crazy!

91 Some people believe pyramids have weird powers. For example, Madame Vasso (her real name was Vissiliki Kortesis) had a blue plastic pyramid at her home in London. She claimed she could heal people if they sat underneath it!

Madame Vasso (1939–2005) was a Greek who settled in Britain. She claimed she could "see" the future, and people visited her to have their fortunes told.

INVESTIGATE

Use the Internet to find out why some pyramid experts were so sure that the hills in Bosnia were actually pyramids of a forgotten people.
Does any real evidence exist?

92 In the 1960s and 1970s, Karel Drbal convinced a lot of people that a pyramid could sharpen razor blades! According to Drbal, a blunt razor blade placed inside a small cardboard or plastic pyramid and left overnight, would be sharp again in the morning. He believed this was because of a pyramid's special shape. Other enthusiasts put fresh food inside pyramid models, because they claimed that this stopped the food from going bad!

93 The author Erich von Däniken wrote in the 1960s that the Giza pyramids were built with the help of aliens! He said humans could not possibly have built such huge buildings using muscle power alone. He worked out that if humans had built the three Giza pyramids it would have taken them at least 664 years. Someone – or something – must have helped them, so von Däniken came up with the idea of alien builders!

The "pyramids" of Bosnia in Eastern Europe, are nothing more than natural hills – but some people are convinced they are real pyramids built by an ancient unknown civilization!

94
In a 19th century cemetery in Europe or North America you might see mini-pyramids. People were fascinated by ancient Egypt, and when they died some had pyramid monuments put over their graves. At Brightling, Sussex, England is the 20-foot-high pyramid tomb of John (Jack) Fuller. It was said that he was buried sitting at a table, with a bottle of wine and wearing a top hat. No wonder he was called "Mad Jack"!

95
"Pyramidology" is alive and well today. In 2006, it was claimed that a group of massive "pyramids" had been discovered in Bosnia. It seemed incredible that no one had spotted them sooner. The discovery made headlines around the world, and a lot of archaeologists laughed. The so-called pyramids were not pyramids at all, but hills that just happened to be pyramid shaped!

Who would have thought that an English country churchyard would be the location for a pyramid? It was built for Mad Jack Fuller in 1834.

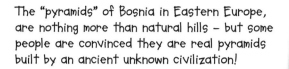

96 **The pyramid shape has inspired architects across the globe.** At Galveston, Texas, the Rainforest Pyramid is a glass conservatory environment for rainforest plants and animals. The architect chose a pyramid shape as it gives the most light.

98 **Since 1970, the Glastonbury festival has been held in fields at Pilton, Somerset, England.** It's a major outdoor music festival, where bands play to thousands of people. The biggest bands play on the Pyramid Stage – a stage covered by a tall, smooth-sided pyramid that's open on one side. Over the years the stage has been rebuilt several times – but it's always been in a pyramid shape!

97 **There's a pyramid at the headquarters of the Summum Organization, in Salt Lake City, Utah.** Summum is a modern religion that offers people the chance to have their dead bodies mummified. The pyramid is used in a ceremony that's meant to help the person's spirit travel to the next life. It's also used as a winery – a place where wine is made!

Pop goes the pyramid – the Pyramid Stage at the Glastonbury music festival, England.

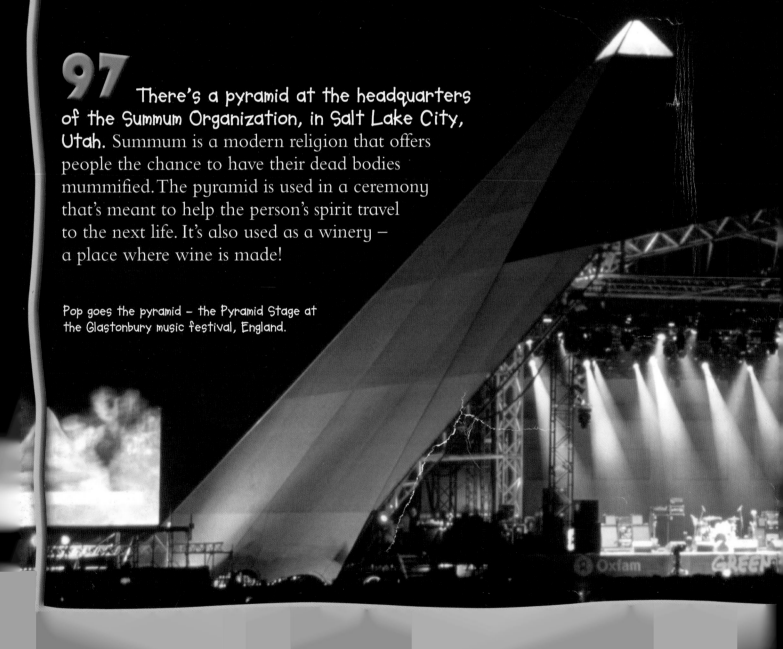

100

The Transamerica Pyramid, in San Francisco, California, looks like a stretched pyramid. It is a 48-story-high skyscaper that points more than 850 feet into the sky. Built in the 1970s, it is designed to be earthquake-proof. If an earthquake shakes San Francisco, the pyramid will rock from side to side but won't come tumbling down.

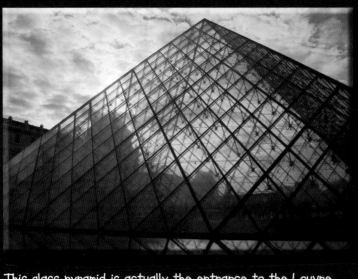

This glass pyramid is actually the entrance to the Louvre museum in Paris, France.

99

The best-known glass pyramid is in Paris, France. The Louvre pyramid, built in the 1980s, is a modern entrance to the world-famous museum. It has 673 panes of glass, and is about 65 feet high. When it was new, lots of people said it spoiled the museum, as the museum's other buildings are all old. Today, it's a must-see building, and it has become a symbol of Paris.

The Transamerica Pyramid is a multi-story office block in San Francisco, USA.

Index

Entries in **bold** refer to main subject entries. Entries in *italics* refer to illustrations.

48

6-12
d
C.D.